Island Press Publishing
P.O. Box 951 Puunene, Hawaii 96784
E-mail: Lisa @ IslandPress. net
WWW. Maradro Island. com

Maradro Island®

Originally published in 1997 in Hawaii by Island Press Publishing.
Printed with soy inks on acid free recycled paper.

Library of Congress Catalogue Number   97-93029

ISBN 0-9656931-0-4

Second United States Edition 1998

MARADRO ISLAND

PASSPORT TO PEACE

WHERE PLANTS and ANIMALS are FREE!

This Book
is
dedicated to
Mother
Earth
on
EARTHDAY
22 april

To Radman and Romeo
and all the Plants,
Animals and Children
in the whole wide world.

Hurt Not the EaRth,
Neither the Sea,
NoR the TREES . . .

Revelations 7:3

HEEEEEELO!
My name is
PApa Papaya!

WELcome to Maradro Island! WE have BEEN waiting for YOU!
I am soooⓞⓞⓞⓞⓞⓞⓞ·ⓞ·ⓞⓞⓞⓞⓞⓞⓞⓞⓞⓞⓞⓞⓞⓞⓞⓞⓞ happy :ÿöü: are HERE!
ⓞⓞⓞⓞⓞⓞⓞⓞⓞⓞⓞⓞⓞⓞⓞⓞⓞⓞⓞⓞⓞⓞⓞⓞh La¨ La Oh Baby BABy!
THErE are many stories told about different Islands in the
world, howeVEr Maradro Island is UNiQUE and I will tell you why.
Maradro Island is a SPECiaL Place that LiVES in HaRmony with
BEautifUL wonderfUL NatUrE. It is a place where plants
and animals talk, And pEople Listen. WiLD Life and TREES are SaFE.
THErE is No FEAR on Maradro IsLand because PEace exists in the
Hearts of ALL! On Maradro IsLand the AiR is clean bEcause
our cars are powErED with WatEr. Our watER is PUrE BEcausE WE
do Not UsE chemicals oR PESticides. This is the REason I am HERE!
I AM a PAPaya FRUit born in the TROPics, and I have made sure
My family has ALWays bEEN 100% organically grown! WELL, one day
I hEard through the GrapEVine that WE WErE going to Be spraxed with
pesticides! There was No Way I could watch my friends aND family
GEt sick and lose the Quality of their LIVES, so I started SEArching
for HEALthy CleaN Land. I began TRaVELing in September of 1992.
Not long after that, I disc-oVErED Maradro IsLand!

While visiting one of the villages, I met a Wise Man who FARMS organically. He said chemicals and pesticides poison the world. He told me there are billions of pounds of pesticides used each year, and less than one percent reaches a pest! Then he told me about life on Maradro Island! How EVERY plant, animal and person work together to keep Mother Earth ALIVE.... For a healthy planet Now, and an EVEN Healthier World for FUTURE generations! At that moment, I knew my search was over. I decided to transplant my family immediately, and we have been here ever since! This is the story of a day in the LIfe of Maradro Island! As YOU take this journey you will meet many of my friends. Some were born here, and some came to ESCAPE the environmental tragedies that the world finds itself in today. YOU get to EXPLORE our ways and join my two favorite friends, Radman and Romeo, on Maradro Island!

HAVE FUN!
LOVE,
PAPA Papaya

P.S. Before you begin, go to your favorite place. Maybe it is in a tree with your PET! Or on a BIG Rock sitting by a stream.... Or is it on a boat in the OCEAN reading IN Bed by CandleLight? Perhaps it is BY the OCEAN under Zillions of Stars reading by the Light of the Moon! Or maybe it is in your bedroom! Just make sure you Love where you are!

P.S.S. I have sent a Letter to Radman and Romeo, via Rosie the Moluccan Cockatoo. (You can read it if you want to.) They have been on a Voyage planting TREES in the RAINFOREST and helping Animals in danger.

Dear Radman and Romeo,
More animals have arrived on Maradro Island.
Four Birds flew in last night. Two from an Oil Spill,
and two barely escaped a Rainforest Fire.
We put Aloe Vera plants on their Burns.
They are healing miraculously!
Also, the Sea Lions found a baby Sea Turtle
entangled in a net by their cave. They said
more are coming!
Please bring at least 100 feet of strong rope.
You have to repel off the steep mountain on
the North Shore.

We miss both of you,
HURRY HOME!!!!!!!
Love,
Papa Papaya

maradro
Island

Papa Papaya
Peace Place
Maradro Island

Radman and Romeo
Green Sea Turtle Route S.P.
approximate Latitude: 105°
approximate Longitude: 108°

Romeo speaks about Radman

He is young and confident, knowing that to be aware of Mother Earth
We must pay attention to what is happening. And Radman knows what is
happening. . . The World is becoming polluted and full of destructive
habits that humans have to break.

His Journeys are filled with Great Observation and Reflection
of what is going on around him.

When he Learned that half of all plants, animals and insects
Live in the Rainforest, Radman started traveling all over the World
to study the interrelationships with each one.

He Lives in the Rainforests along with Plants, Animals and people,
Seeing how each one depends on the Existence of one another.

His compassion grows constantly for Mother Earth, as he watches
how she provides a home for Each and every species.

Radman sees the plan Mother Nature has created, and knows
that through Silent Observation, We can Learn the Secret
to a harmonious Life. . .

The Journey

"This is where Papa Papaya said the Sea Turtles are!
Romeo, Climb Down the mountain as fast as you can,
and I will meet you on Shore!"

"Radman! There are about eight new Sea Turtles
that just arrived...They are tangled in Nets!"

"Romeo, Swim with me! We will take the
Rope out to the Turtles, then help
me Pull them in!"

Romeos View of the Sea Turtle
while Swimming into Shore.

The Arrival of the Sea Turtle

Sea turtles have roamed for MILLIONS of years,
NOW is the time to LISTEN and HEAR!
ALL Eight Species are going EXTINCT,
it is SERIOUS trouble, MORE than WE think!
Their SURVIVAL is important in and out of the Sea,
Can you hear them Calling, "Please LET us SWIM FREE!"
"Watch out for the Jellyfish!" one turtle says to another,
"It could be a Plastic Bag, and if you SWALLOW it,
that would be DISASTROUS!"
They are POISONED by Pollution and Strangled by trash,
if that's not ENough, some people capture them for CASH!
Humans take their EGGS and SELL their LEATHER,
This is WHY WE Have to Get together and tell the Masses,
Not to BUY TURTLE products or tortoise shell glasses!
The SEA TURTLES SURVIVAL Depends on You and ME,
Let us HELP them by CLEANING Up the SEA!
Then at Last they can SWIM free,
and ALL ocean Life WILL LIVE PEACEFULLY!

Did you know Sea Turtles have been around for 200 million years? There are Eight species of Sea Turtles roaming the World today! Green Sea Turtle, Black Sea Turtle, Leatherback, Olive Ridley, Kemp's Ridley, Hawksbill, Loggerhead, and the Australian Flatback. When Sea Turtles swim, they surface to breathe every few minutes. When they are resting, the Sea Turtle can stay under water for as Long as 2½ hours!

Sea Turtles Live most of their Lives in the Ocean, however female turtles must come up to the Beach to Lay her eggs. She instinctively goes back to the same beach where she was born. This is where she will Lay 100 Eggs! The female Turtle covers the nest with sand and returns to the Sea.

After 60 days, the eggs hatch and the baby Sea Turtles race to the Ocean where they will swim and swim and swim and swim! The Sea Turtle's favorite food is jellyfish. Sometimes the Turtle eats plastic bags, thinking they are jellyfish!

The Green Sea Turtles that made it to Maradro Island, remind us that ALL TURTLES are at Risk of going Extinct because of hunting and polluted waters.

In the American Indian Tradition the Turtle represents 'Keeper of the Earth'. Maradro Island's Sea Turtles ask, "Can you help my friends and family by cleaning up beaches, cutting six pack plastic rings, Recycling as much as you can, and never ever buy Turtle products!"

Simon the Smart Sea Otter says, "Put on your wet suit and goggles and follow me into the Deep blue Sea!"

Swimming and playing WAS the name of their game,
UNTIL one day the POLLUTION came...
Covered with OIL and PESTICIDES from SOIL,
the SEA LIONS started SEARCHING for CLEAN WATER!
They SWAM and SWAM until they SWAM into
Simon the SMART SEA OTTER!
Simon said, "WE are DYING FROM POLLUTION,
however I do have a SOLUTION,
Just WEAR a WET SUIT and goggles!
Put them on and FOLLOW ME,
to a BEAUTIFUL Ocean where YOU can SWIM FREE!
Watch out for BOTTLES and OIL and TRASH,
and if you SWIM into NETS that catch,
SLIDE down to the End, there is an ESCAPE hatch!
Keep FOLLOWING me into the DEEP BLUE SEA,
I will show YOU an ISLAND that LIVES in harmony!
They do not have NETS, there is No OIL,
or PESTICIDE RUN OFF FROM the SOIL.
There ARE No CHEMICALS or ARTIFICIAL PLASTIC,
Because on MARADRO ISLAND,
EVErybody KNOWS that would be Catastrophic!
Can You IMAGINE When the WORLD AGREES
To Stop DUMPING Waste into the Sea?
Fish will be HEALThy, Whales and DoLphins WILL SURVIVE,
and the WHOLE food chain would LIVE Thriving Lives!
There are small things that WE CAN Do,
to Stop POLLUTION and HELP Animals too!
EAT ORGANIC food to CLean up the SoiL,
and Ride your Bike to Reduce the OiL
Use products that are CHEMICAL FREE,
So harmful POLLUtants do not END UP in the Sea!
When we become AWARE and everyone starts GIVing
We will have a WORLD that will continue LIVing!
LET US make SURE Mother Earth stays Healthy,
Then PLANET EARTH will surely be wealthy!

Do you know the difference between Sea Lions and Seals?
Sea Lions have EXTERNAL EARS, and SEALS have EARS that are
STREAMLINED to make them faster swimmers!
Sea Lions are the divers! They DIVE to depths of 450 feet
(138m), and stay submerged for up to TWENTY minutes!
There are five species of Sea Lions.
The Stellar, Californian, South American, Australian,
and the NEW Zealand Sea Lion.
The LARGEST of the Sea Lions is the Stellar. The Male weighs
a TON and females weigh about 595 pounds (270 kilograms).
They inhabit Pacific beaches, from the Aleutian Islands of
Alaska to Japan.
California Sea Lions Love to LIVE in Caves around the
coast of California and the Galapagos Islands.
You can find the South American Sea Lion from PERU
around Cape Horn to Uruguay.
Australian Sea Lions Love to SLeep and spend their LIVES
at the Beach, where they are born.
NEW Zealand Sea Lions are Island Lovers!
Maradro Island's New Zealand Sea Lions Remind us to
Love EVERything WE do, then WE can Experience the
Beauty of the Moment!

There are two kinds of Otters... The River Otter and the Sea Otter. The Sea Otter lives in the North Pacific Ocean from California to Alaska and the Aleutian Islands. They also live in the waters off the Northeastern part of the Soviet Union.

Sea Otters are the LARGEST of ALL Otters. They grow over 4 feet (1.2 meters) in length, and weigh over 80 pounds (36 kilograms).

The River Otters include the Giant Brazilian from South America, the Eurasian Otter from Europe, North Africa, Asia and Japan. Oriental Small claw lives in India, the African small claw and African Clawless are in Africa, the American River Otter lives in North America, Alaska and Canada, the Hairy Nose Otter is from Southern Asia, and the Smooth Coated Otters live in Southeast Asia.

Making slides in the mud and having fun is River Otters favorite thing to do! They spend hours sliding down hills in mud or snow, playing with rocks and sticks along the way!

Sea Otters chase each other as they jump and swim over waves, diving to depths of up to 1300 feet (400 meters) without surfacing to breathe! Both the River Otter and the Sea Otter are very affectionate and playful! In the American Indian tradition, the Otter represents Joy and Laughter. Simon the Sea Otter asks, "What have you laughed about lately?"

Bon Jour! Oh hi my friend! My name is Clawdia!
It is ALWAYS fun to be at Hattie's Café on Wednesdays!
That is when Milo the Alligator brings in fresh pizza from
the other side of the Island! Mmmmm, that reminds me of the
first time I arrived on Maradro Island...

I was in the Caribbean somewhere between Martinique
and St. Barth, dancing to the heartbeat of Island Life,
when I heard about a New Restaurant that was looking for
Fresh Live Crabs! I immediatly imagined sitting on a plate, next
to a Lemon, listening to French music, waiting for my Life to
End! That was it. I went back to my Rock, packed my
Castanettes and started crossing Ocean after Ocean.

One day I found myself Entangled in a Driftnet with
a Dolphin. I was helping my new friend Escape, (by sawing
the net with my claw) when all of a sudden he said,
"Shhh, Listen! It is a whale singing a song!" I Listened
intently to his Melodic Music. A peaceful feeling came
over me like Never before... He was singing about an
Island that Lives in Peace. It turned out to be
Maradro Island! I can still remember his song...

♫ We express our Joy by making a Splash,
but driftnets and whaling ships are upon our path!
We are hunted by humans for Oil and Meat,
Now we are slowly going Extinct...
We must Leave the Commercial Zone,
and I know an Island we can call home!
Maradro Island is the place to Be,
if You want to Live a Life that is Free! ♫

When I heard his song, I knew I was headed in the
Right Direction! YES!

I arrived Late one night when the Moon was full.
All I could see was a Little hut high in the Mountains.
The Moon Lit up a sign that said "Milos Pizza".
I looked around and it was the most Beautiful place
that I had Ever Seen!

I must admit, I was still a little scared about
Ending up in Crab Pasta or something!

CRABS are CRUSTACEANS . . . A soft body protected by a hard shell.
all crustaceans have jointed appendages. That means two pair of antennae,
and a hard exoskeleton.
There are over 50,000 species of Crustaceans! The groups of crustaceans
include Copepods, Barnacles, Shrimp, Lobster and Crabs.
You can find most Crabs at the Beach, although some crabs live in River Water.
What happens when you grab a crab by one Leg? They will probably pinch you,
but the crab could be in the mood to drop one of his Legs so he can get away!
It is their way of protecting themselves from getting hurt! But don't worry,
the Crabs Leg is Replaced by a Remarkable process called Regeneration.
That means they can easily grow a new Leg to replace the one they Let go of!
Clawdia, the Red Crab, has observed Hermit Crabs in her travels. She has noticed
hermit crabs find shells that are Empty, and hang out until the shell gets too small.
Then as the Crabs grow, they find new shells that fit perfect!
Clawdia reminds us that when our shell gets too small, or does not feel quite right,
don't be afraid to 'Let go' of the one we have, and find another that fits Just Right!

Dolphins Love to BE with FRIENDS and FAMiLy! They Live in groups of twenty to one hundred.

Most dolphins grow from 4-14 feet (1.2-2.4 meters), and weigh between 50-500 pounds (23-225 kilograms).

HERE are Some of the Dolphins that are Swimming the World's oceans today . . .

Boto and TUCUZi Live in the Amazon, Indus and Ganges River Dolphin swim in Pakistan and India, the VaQuita is in Mexico, Baiji Dolphin is from China, HECtoRS Dolphin swims the shores of New Zealand, Humpbacked and spotted Dolphins aRE in the Atlantic Ocean, Franciscana Lives in South america, and both Bottlenose and Spinner Dolphin CRUISE around the PACific Ocean.

EvERy Dolphin has their own individual whistle. He can call another dolphin friend by imitating her whistle! Dolphins can Also communicate through their Rounded foreheads called MELons.

You can hear them for up to a mile away!

Did you know the Lower jawbone is Really an ULTRaSENSITIVE EaR that the Dolphins hear with?

A mother Dolphin gives birth to one baby at a time. Other dolphins surround the mother when she is giving birth, and help by pulling her tail. The dolphins stay with the Mother to protect the new baby, Keeping it safe from harm. Injured and Sick dolphins are ALWays caRED for by fRiends and family.

Dolphins Live their LIVES in JoYful harmony with Each other and their WoRLD. They PLAY and Love!

Some people think Dolphins are more intelligent than humans. What do you think?

Dolphins know the Lesson of LOVE, and that it is the most important part of LIFE!

MaRadRo IsLand's Dolphin's touch You and Ask, "Can you help your FRIEND's and family in times of NEED?"

The BLUE WHALE is the LARGEST animal that has EVER LIVED on EARTH!
THEY grow up to 100 FEET in LeNGTH (31m), and weigh more than 250 toNS!
As many as 30 LARGE ELephants!
WhaLes have been here since the Beginning of the Age of Mammals
more than 45 MilLion yEARS ago!
Did you know that Whales, DoLphiNS, and porpoises make up a special
group called "Cetacea". Cetaceans are divided into toothed WhaLES
and Baleen WHALES. The DiffERENCE is how they Eat their fooD.
When BaLEEN WhaLES are HuNGRY, they just open up their mouth,
and their combLike teeth filter or strain plankton and small fish
as they CRUISE through the SeaWATER. TootHED WHALES Eat LARger
Sea MammaLS AND have to CHASE their pREY.
The BaLeeN WhaLES are the BLue WHALE, Humpback Whale, GREY,
Brydes WhaLE, Sei WhaLE, FiN, Pigmy Right WhaLE, Right WhaLE,
(Pigmy's are Smaller) BowheaD and Minke.
The TootHED WhaLes incLuDe the KiLLeR WhaLe, FaLse KiLLer WhaLe,
Short FiNNED PiLot. Long FiNNeD PiLot, the BELuga (White WhaLE),
NaRwhaL, Pygmy SPERM WhaLe, Sperm WhaLe, CUViERS BeaKed WHaLe,
BaiRDS BeaKED Whale and the BottLeNose WhaLe.
The Humpback WHaLe grows as LoNG as 46 fEET (14m) and weighs
40 toNS (36,000k).
Humpbacks cRUISE ALaska Waters in the SuMMER months, Where they
fEED, then the GentLe GiaNts move to WARmeR tropicaL oceaNS in the
WiNTeR, wheRe they mate and give BiRTH. This is a Happy time
for the WHaLe! They sHow theiR EmotioNS By BREEChing.
(Jumping in the AiR), taiL sLapping, anD SingiNG songs!
Humpbacks are known for their 180° meLoDies. Some Scientists
think their songs compaRe to Human CLassicaL compositioNS!
WhaLEs have an iNtuitive nature that pEopLe have too!
MaRaDRo IsLaND's Humpback WhaLe, SUNNY, asks, "Are you in
touch with your intuitive Nature?" It comes from the stiLL
smaLL voicE Deep INSIDE. Your intuitive nature knows EvERYthing!

Radman, what is DEEP ECOLOGY?
WELL ROMEO, it is a philosophy where Humans
are EQUALLY important to EVERY OTHER SPECIES.
WE MUST ALLOW other SPECIES to FOLLOW THEIR
OWN EVOLUTIONARY DESTINIES without
INTERFERING with THEM.

Welcome to My little Café!
I hope you like My MENU today!
My name is Hattie and I don't eat meat
because YOU SEE, I have a BELIEF...
Do Unto Others as YOU Would have them do Unto You,
Maradro Island's Plants, Animals and People LIVE Like this too!
I am here to SERVE Mother EARTH, and NOW,
Right now, I WILL speak My TRUTH!
Eating meat is Linked to disease,
My Message to YOU is, don't Eat it please!
It's not GOOD for our BODIES, Souls or Minds,
Let's Stop hurting the Animals and just Be kind!
Not eating meat would bring PROfound changes,
The Rainforests could LIVE without harmful danger!
It would save precious WATER and Re-Balance Nature,
Then WE Would have a healthy future!
WE could GROW tons of Grain and feed the hungry,
Lower fossil fuel and help Earth's Soil!
Now if YOU want to FEEL ALiVe,
Eat fruits, grains and Vegetables that Nature provides!
To Be healthy, Nature GIVES US these Foods,
When WE eat this Way, WE WILL all feel Good!
So Remember, next time someone offers You meat,
Think about Mother Earth and Living in Peace!

Love and KISSES,

Hattie

Hatties distant relatives.
The Hula Kula Cows.

ALLigator ALLigator, Crocodile CRocodiLe,
How can I teLL you apart? First you SEE My little COOKIE,
Look at CrocodiLes SMiLe to start!
His teeth are Exposed when his mouth is cLoseD,
and my TEEth? I hide them weLL!
Put us together side by side,
Look at my nose, it is short and wide
and CRocodiLes NOSE is Longer than mine!
We have a family of twenty nine SPECIES,
Yet VERY FEW Remain....
PLEase Ask hunters to Stop Hurting us
if killing is theIR GameE!
Listen to this if you want to know
how BIG our SPECIES can get,
then PLEase teLL me honestly
if you would Like CrocodiLE oR I as a pEt?!
CRocodiLES grow to be a thousand pounds,
And a record breaking thirty four FEET IN Length,
and As you probabLy Already know,
He has incredible STRENGTH!
And I, the aLLiGator,
fuLL GRown we wEIgh 500 pounds
and up to Nineteen FEEt,
Now if You aRE standing up, PLEase have a seat!
I used to EAT anything IN front of Me,
at least thats the way it USED to BE....
UntiL I Met a GirL named LiZa,
Who Cooked me a Vegetarian PIZZa!
It was Soooooooooooo●OOOO●●●●●● GooD!
As I took another Bite,
I began to SEE things in a NEW Light!
I finished my delicious PIZZa,
then swam the swamps DEEP in thought....
I no LoNGER wanted to Live IN FEAR of being caught!
So I went on the Road And foLLoweD my Heart,
I knew I was headed for a brand new stARt!
My imagination was in FRont of Me,
I watcheD it unfold into My destiny!
Going DeepeR into my dREAM,
I was SEEING ALL kinds of things!
I saw a Hut high IN the Mountains
on A WonderfuL little IsLaND!
Then it flASHeD Right before Me,
"MiLos PIZZa" on a SIGN,
it turned out my DREAM was REALity the whole time!
I have New friends that had the same intention,
they moved out of SURViVaL mode and probable EXtiNctioN!
Thank God we made it to Maradro IsLand!
Now we ARE happy as can be,
to Live our NEW Life CompleteLy FREe!
WHen we move away from FeaR,
the puRPoSE of LiFe becomes so cLear!
Let us create a chain reaction
to GiVe EVERybody ComPLEte satisfaction!
Do ALL you can for EARths pLants, ANimaLs and MAN,
THen wiLL everything become ONE?
Can you GUESS?

        I Say YES!
     Love and kisses,
      and whippedcREAM!

        MiLo the ALLigator

Alligators and Crocodiles have been on Earth since the Great Age of Reptiles, 225 to 65 million years ago! They are the Survivors of the Dinosaur days! There is another animal that is closely related to Alligators and Crocodiles. It is called a "Gavial". Gavials have a Longer and Thinner snout than the Crocodile. He swims around the Malay Peninsula in Sumatra and Borneo, India. Have you heard of the False Gavial? He is his own species, classified by himself. Alligators, Crocodiles, Caimans, False Gavial and Gavials make up a group called "Crocodilians". Together there are twenty nine species.

The American Alligator is home in the Southeastern United States, and the Chinese Alligator lives in the Yangtze River in China.

Caimans (Broad snouted, Rio apaporif, Spectacle, Brown, Black, Cuviers Dwarf and Smooth fronted) make their home in South America. Johnstons and the Salt Water Crocodile live from India to Northern Australia. Nile Crocodiles live in Africa along with the African Dwarf, Congo Dwarf, Slender snouted Crocodile, and the Sharp nose Crocodile. The Cuban Crocodile swim the swamps of Cuba. The Mugger is in India and Pakistan, New Guinea Crocodile lives in New Guinea, Siamese lives in Thailand and Indonesia. The Mindoro live near the Phillipine Islands, American Crocodile lives in Southern Florida, the Ceylonese live in Ceylon, and the Orinoco are in the Rivers of South America. The Morlets live in Central America, the River Crocodile in Columbia and you can find the Jacare Crocodile in Paraguay.

A Mother Alligator Lays between 30-50 eggs. She builds her Nest at Night and uses Leaves, Mud and Sand. It takes several nights to make this three foot (1 meter) nest. Mother Crocodiles will only Lay her eggs in Saltwater, and can Lay up to 100 eggs. Both Alligator and Crocodile Mothers stay by the Nest to protect the eggs until they hatch in two or three months. Baby crocodiles have a special "egg tooth" for breaking their shell while they hatch.

At about 5 or 6 years old, Alligators and Crocodiles are Adults! In the American Indian Culture, the Alligator represents the power to Survive! Milo, the American Alligator asks, "Are you taking good care of yourself by Exercising and Eating Food that makes you feel Strong and healthy?" He reminds us to choose foods that will Nourish us, So we will be Ready for any situation!

To LIVE in an Aware and Loving state
one must Accept and Understand all paths
that we cross. Listen to EVERyonE.
We all have our own story.

My Story is one that comes from EMPATHY
For ALL my friends and FAMILY....
I can not stand to SEE animals fall victim
into human hands wanting only to shoot them!
Just to hang us in a store,
or in someone's house above the DOOR!
I knew what OBVIOUSLY had to happen,
A change in CONCIOUSNESS for those who want them!
Some people kill Animals for sport and profit,
this is something I have Learned,
I wonder how humans would feel if the tables were turned?
My Friend Elephant found a BULLET proof VEST,
Tried it on wanting to SEE if it Fit,
He thought we could wear them for self preservation,
it was our only hope of possible Salvation!
However, this VEST was not for us to wear,
The REAL ISSUE was THIS:
We did not want to RUN and HIDE in FEAR,
Everytime A Human being came near!
So ALL of our FRIENDS joined together and DECIDED what to Do,
We wanted to FIND a PLACE for THREATENED ANIMALS to come to!
When we became clear about our NEW direction,
That is when we met Romeo and Radman!
This is How it HAPPENED....
I FELT the URGE to CLIMB A PALM TREE,
Looked through my TELESCOPE And what did I see?
Radman and Romeo coming toward me!
On a TURTLE in the ocean,
They were Approaching LAND with the Wind in Motion!
Upon the SHORE they SAID to us,
"There is a PEACEFUL ISLAND you can come to If you wish!
Gather your FRIENDS and A whole bunch of seeds,
Because on Maradro ISLAND we love to plant TREES!
We are traveling the World letting Animals know,
They will be SAFE on Maradro!"
We KNEW our DREAM was coming TRUE,
Now I ASK you, "Are your Dreams coming TRUE too?

The SIBERIAN TIGER is the most powerful in the cat family!
Male Tigers Reach a Length of 11 feet (3.4m.), and weigh up to
650 pounds (295 Kg.). Females are usually smaller, about
nine feet (2.8m.) Long, and weigh 400 pounds (182 Kg.).
Did you know three feet (.92m.) of their nine foot body is
all tail?

At the beginning of the twentieth century there were Eight
species of Tiger's in the World. Can you name them?
Siberian, Indian, Javan, Indonesian-Chinese, Caspian, Chinese-
Manchurian, the Balinese, and the Sumatran Tiger.
There are very few Tiger's left in the Wild.
Some species are threatend, some are Endangered and
four species are now Extinct. (Caspian, Chinese-Manchurian,
Javan and Balinese.)
We must protect the Remaining Species by never buying
Animal skins from the Tiger or any other animal!
Maradro Island's Indian Tiger, Antoñio, (who dyed his
stripes purple) asks, "are You Expressing your Creativity?"
When we Live a Life of unexpressed creativity, it is
because we are Living somebody Else's truth, and not our own.
When Antoñio started Living his truth, and not what he was
Expected to do, (his family members expected him to hunt
prey all day, Everyday!) he chose to paint purple pastel
paintings and even designed the Purple Palm Palace
in India. His talent goes on and on. If he Lived someone
Else's truth, he would not be the Great Artist he is today!
What is your Creativity? What do you Love doing more
than anything in the World? Imagination happens when
you actually begin your creative work.

Purple Palm Palace.

Little Elephant went to a New School
where teaching PEACE was IN,
then and there right where WE were
was when it ALL Began!
Toy guns and weapons were Never used
not even for outside PLAY,
How can pEace on Earth exist
when killing is going on Everyday?
What path to take, there are so Many,
how do you know which Road to journey?
Listen to your voice within and know,
What you do today Effects tomorrow!
Follow your heart with Love and Joy,
then watch things happen the harmonious way!
Be true to yoursELf, so be it with others,
accept everyone as sister and Brother!
Live and Let Live is Easy to say,
practice by accepting Everybodies way!
Show by example, there is nothing to pReach,
Just Live your own Life with happiness and peace!
Look within and you will find your outside world reflection
For what WE think, we will create,
Make sure it is a positive direction!
Anything that hurts another is negative play in action,
Unhappiness comes as a result, causing dissatisfaction!
So stop the play of guns and weapons
then watch Excitement grow,
When we Live the positive ways,
WE will have a hEalthy tomorrow!

THERE ARE TWO DIFFERENT KINDS of ELEPHANTS LIVING IN THE WORLD TODAY. . . . .
THE AFRICAN ELEPHANT and tHE INDIAN ELEPHANT. THEY ARE THE LARGEST of ALL Land ANimals!
THE BIGGEST is tHE African Elephant. He STANDS 14 FEET TALL (5 meTerS), AND WEIGHS AS MUCH as
22,000 POUNDS (9,979 KiLograms).

THE INDIAN ELEPHANT is smaller THAN THE African ELEPHANT. He WEiGHS ABouT 11,000 POUNDS
(5,000 KiLograms), AND His HEIGHT is ALmost 10 FEET (3meTers).

ALL ELEPHANTS ARE VEGETARIANS. THEy EAT about 400 POUNDS (182 KiLograms) of FRUIT,
LEaVES AND BRANCHES A DAY!

ELEPHANTS LIVE IN FAMILy TRoops of BETWEEN 10-50 ANimals, aND ARE USUALLY LED By A mature female.
DID yOU KNOW FEMALE ELEPHANTS ARE CALLED COWS? MALE ELEPHANTS ARE CalLED BULLS oR TUSKERS,
AND YOUNG ELepHants are CALLED CALVES.

Do yoU KNOW ABouT tHE SECRET LANGUAGE of ELEPHANTS? THERE ARE MaNY SOUNDS tHAT ELephants
CAN HEAR, AND HUMANS CaNNot. THat is BECAUSE some of tHEIR SouNDS ARE BELoW ouR
RANGE of HEARING, IN WHat is KNOWN AS 'INFRaSOUNDS'. EARTH is fULL of InFRaSOUND.
It is GENERATED By WIND, tHUNDER, VoLCANoES aND oCEAN STorMS. It is MaSSiVE moVeMENTS of
EARTH, AiR, FiRE aND WaTer.

INFRaSOUND LETS tHE ELEPHANTS cOMMUNICATE oVER LONG DistaNces. THis is How MaLE
ELepHants FinD FEMaLES IN BREEDING CoNDitioN.

THe femaLE ELEPHANT SINGS HER SoNG WItH inFRasounD FREQUeNCIES, AND SOON,
MaLE ELEPHaNTS COME FRom ALL DIRECTiONS!

FemaLE GesTation PERIod LASTS tWo YEARS, aND AFTeR tHE Baby eLEphant is BoRN,
it ReMains witH its MotHer FoR ANotHER tWo YEARS.

MARaDRo ISLaND'S ELEPHANT, CLAY, TELLS A STorY ABouT a LittLe eLEphant tHAt Goes to
a SCHOOL WHERE CHILDREN Do Not WaNT to HuRT otHERS. He REMiNDS US Now,
tHat tHE PERSoN WHo UpSets US tHE MoSt is oNE of ouR GREATEST tEACHERS!

INSTEAD of WANTiNG to HURT tHE PERSoN WHo TRIGGERS ouR ANGER, WE mUST Look INSIDE
to SeE WHat is HuRTiNg US. By ENTeRING OUR PAiN, WE WILL GAIN EVEN mORE STRENGtH
AND BECome EVEN STRONGER! THEN WE CAN HELP PEoPLE, iNSTEaD of HuRTING tHEM.

Almost All of Africa's Elephants will be gone in twenty years if the present killing rate continues. Ten years ago there were 1.5 Million Elephants in Africa. Today, because of culling and Slaughtering for their Ivory, they may become extinct by the year 2,000.
Solution: Don't buy Ivory!
Long Live the Elephant!

Excerpt from Elephant World magazine Page 22.

In my Rowboat I contemplate,
What is Going on in the World to Date...
I know About guns that humans carry,
And Between You and Me BABY, it is Very scary!
I will tell you my story and How it happend,
You know, how I ended up on Maradro ISLAND!
I was up in a TREE EAting some Honey,
One clear Day when it was sunny...
I Heard a gunshot from Afar,
Yes, it was time to move once more!
I was Climbing Down about to Run,
When Rosie the Cockatoo flew past the sun!
Her Shadow cast a Perfect Light,
For me to see a wise insight!
Sudden Excitement then came to me,
And as I Awoke, I Began to see...

FORGET the guns and the WARS,
Then WATCH PEACE walk through the Door...
Harmony is what nature intends,
Perfect BALance can then Begin!
Follow Your Heart and Just Be kind,
to Every PLANT, Animal and Person you find!

As it turned out, Rosie came to SAY,
"Come with me to Maradro ISLAND today!"
I Rowed and Rowed then Came Ashore,
to Exquisite nature and so much More!
We on Maradro want to Share with You,
Our Alive Lifestyle, So How Do you Do?!
We Have our WAY's to HELP Mother EARTH,
And know HER Cycle of Giving BIRTH...
We Do not Have guns Because they kill,
the Purpose of our Lives is to fulfill!
Give And give ALL that we can,
to Mother EARTH's Plants, Animals and MAN!
It is so GOOD to Be Alive, Happy And Free,
Now I Understand, Giving and Forgiving
Are two of the Keys!

There are Nine Species of BEARS hanging out around the World today!
The KODIAK BEAR, BROWN Bear, North American Black Bear, Asiatic Black Bears,
Polar Bears, Sloth Bear, Spectacled Bear, Malayan Sun Bear, and Teddy Bear.
The BIGGEST and STRONGEST BEAR is the KODIAK BEAR. He measures Nine Feet
Eight inches TALL (three meters), and weighs more than any other Bear, One thousand
seven hundred pounds! (Seven hundred fifty five kg.)
They LIVE on KODIAK Island in the Gulf of ALaska, and are Also found on the
Islands of Afognak and Shuxak.
You can find BROWN BEARS in the Mountains of North America. When they
are in the ROCKy Mountain wilderness, they are Called GRIZZLY Bears,
and when they are in Inland Alaska, Canada and Russia they are called
BROWN BEARS. They are the FASTEST Runners, Running at speeds of fourty
Eight kilometers (Thirty miles per hour)!
North American Black Bears are found in Mexico, California, the Great Lakes
and Newfoundland.
Asiatic Black Bears are Sometimes called Moon Bears or Himalayan Bears.
They Live in the Himalayan Mountains and Love climbing to the TREELINE!
1500 feet (460 meters).
POLAR BEARS are Excellent divers and swimmers! They maintain Speed
for 2 to 3 minutes, then Relax and CRUISE by Riding the Ice FLOES with
the CURRENT, then swim home. They LoVe To TRAVEL Distances!
The SLoth Bear hangs out CLIMBING TREES on the Island of SRI LANKa and
in India. They Like Living in the JUNGLES and Low Dry areas. Some People call
the SLoth Bear, The Indian BEAR.
You can find the SPECTacled Bear high in the Andes mountains in South America.
The Malayan Sun BEAR makes his home in the TREES of Sumatra, Indo-China
and Thailand. He is the Smallest of all Bears, about four feet (one point two meters),
and weighs about One hundred Ten pounds (fifty KG.).
You might think PANDa BeaRS are classified as a Bear, however, Some TAXonomists
(People who classify animal species), think PANDAS are closer to the Raccoon family.
The GIANT PANDa Leads a Solitary Peaceful Life in the Bamboo Forests from China to TIBet.
What about Koala BEARS? They are Classified as Marsupials. They feed at Night on
Eucalyptus Leaves and Live in the TREES in Australia.

The Teddy Bear is the most Loving of all Bears! He will Always Be There for YOU,
no matter what! He is Also one of the BEST Listeners. He always wants to Know how
you are feeling. TALK to Him!
Most Bears spend the Winter in hibernation. At this time Mama Bears have their
Babies. When SPRingtime comes, the Cubs Emerge from the CAVE, Ready to Learn
and PLAY while Exploring NATURE!
In the American Indian Culture, the BEAR represents STRENGTH.
BRaD, the GRIZZLY Bear that made it to MaRaDRO Island, asks, "ARE YOU
Practicing Your Strength and Conviction in Living Your Truth and Doing What
You know to be Right?" Follow Your Heart and KNOW the Power of LoVe!

Imagine when the WORLD LiVES
Without FEAR . . .
Peace WiLL exist in Hearts
EVeRywhere!

As I fly to Maradro Island tonight,
I will tell you my STORY while in flight!
I have flown across oceans and over hills,
finding myself immersed in Oil spills!
I was stuck in oil up to my neck,
Oh Boy, was I a Wreck!
Then one time I remember,
flying to Mexico in mid December...
All of a sudden I started to Choke,
it was Car Exhaust and factory smoke!
Then I was caught in Acid Rain,
it stung my eyes, I was in Pain!
To Wear an Oxygen Mask was the only solution
for all this kind of harmful pollution!
I had to get out, the Air was poison
So I flew back to my original destination!
It felt Good, oh soooooo good to be back in my nest,
Now I could give my Body a Rest!
I came from Brazil deep in the Jungle,
then along came the Rainforest fires,
And that, I just could not handle!
I was tired of Moving from Tree to tree
Every time a Fire came close to me!
I made a Vow and said to myself,
I have to Leave, this is not good for my health!
I was tired and so I took a nap,
When I awoke, My Friend Toucan was holding a Map...
He said," I lost my home today,
its not fun here anymore, We Can't even Play!
I came to tell you another Fire is Near,
Let's take off together and get out of here!"
We looked at the Map and charted our flight,
Then decided to Leave Late that Night...
The Smoke was thick, We could not See,
Our charted Map was history!
We started flying in one direction,
going with our intuition...
We flew and flew until we Landed,
Right in the heart of Maradro Island!
When I think back about my nightmare,
I take a deep Breath and Breathe Clean Air,
I close My eyes and Make a Wish,
That we can All play our Part with Great Mother Earth!
The Ozone is thinning at an Alarming Rate,
We must Repair it before it is too late!
Stop burning Trees, Oil and Fuel,
and Convert to what Mother Nature wants us to use!
She has been here all along,
Her Harmonious way is giving us the Water, Wind and Sun!

Rosie is from the Southern Mollucan Islands in Indonesia, where Cockatoos have Existed for over Ten Thousand years!

Rosie flew to the Carnival in Brazil on her fourth Birthday, then followed her Heart to the Brazilian Rainforest, where she Lived for many Years...That is...Until the Rainforest fires started happening.

Rosie arrived on Maradro Island in May of 1992. This is when she started Living her True Passion for flying! (Rosie flies around the World delivering letters of Urgency to People who can help animals in distress.)

Rosie Asks, "Are you Living your passion?" Give away whatever is holding you back, (fear, worry, judgement, etc.) follow Your heart and Live your Truth with Passion!

There are thirty seven species of Toucans!
They can be found in forests from
Southern Mexico through Central America,
as well as Northern and Eastern parts
of South America.
The Toucan that made it to Maradro Island
is the plate billed Mountain Toucan.
He comes from the Tropical Rainforest in
South America, and can be found in Altitudes
of up to 10,000 feet (3,000 m). He measures
about 17 inches (43 cm). The LARGEST Toucan
is 26 inches (65 cm). ALL Toucans have very
BIG Beaks! about 8 inches (20 cm) Long. They use
their beaks to EAT fruits and berries.
The upper part of the beak is saw toothed.
Toucans play an important role in distributing
seeds throughout the Rainforests.
Maradro Island's Toucan Tom asks, "Can you help
plant Trees and Seeds to make sure animals
Always have their homes?"
You Can! Just Like Toucan!

Helping the forests
helps the plants
and Animals!

ALIVE and Lush, You have ENTERED the FOREST,
Thriving on WEt drenching RAIN . . .
SINGING BIRDS and CHIRPING insects,
Watch the innerplay !
When We stop and LISTEN to the TREES,
You WILL HEAR them whisper, "Help us please !"
RAINFORESTS are disappearing, and it is Happening fast,
EVerybody has Their part to PLAY.
or they WILL Not Last !
We NEED the TREES to SURVIVE,
The AIR they Supply us Gives us our Lives !
This is the Reason We MUST HELP them,
Because, Without the RAINFORESTS, EVERYTHING dies.
TREES CLEAN the AIR, they give us SHADE,
This is Where NaTures BALANCE is made !
PLANTS, ANimals and TRiBes aLIKE,
NEED their Homes for FUTURE Life !
INDUSTRY is CLEARING LAND for Cattle and Timber,
AND Yes, there is something WE MUST Remember . . . .
Decrease Demand and We WILL SEE,
HEALThy, LoNg Living, Life Giving TREES !
Life or death, We have Two choices,
This is When We NEED OUR Voices !
SPEAK UP, Speak up and take a STAND,
Recycle, Recycle for RAINFOREST LAND !
PLANT TREES for Life to flourish,
then Watch NATURE completely nourish !
When we grasp the Life giving Ways,
EARTH WILL BE Peaceful,
and WE WILL LIVE HEALThy Days !

Only after the Last Tree has been cut down,
only after the Last River has been poisoned,
only after the Last fish has been caught,
only then will you find that money cannot be eaten.

CREE Indian Prophecy

FROGGY FROGGIE in the RAIN,
Jumping, SINGing and PLAYing games!
Man came in, Now FROG is out,
of his ELEMENT and her house!
Where to go, he cannot see,
Because of SMOKE From BURNing TREES!
WiLL he go INTo the City?
PLEASE Warn him of the DANGER,
Even if You aRE A Stranger!
Watch out for caRs and moving Trains,
In SUBWAY Stations, hide in the Water drain!
When Silence is PRESENT, Please Come out,
BE Confident and FEARLESS without any doubt!
Look foR ROMEO and hop on his back,
He wiLL be WEARing a PURPLE PACK!
Hold oN TIGHT, Get READY To EXPLORE,
ROMEO wiLL take YOU on a RIDE like NEVER befoRE!
You wiLL cross MOuntains and a FEW STREAMS,
then come upon an Ocean that is VeRy Clean!
KEEP holding on to WONDERFUL ROMEO,
Look straight Ahead, MaRaDRo ISLAND will be in Front of you!
You have ARRIVED at A Place where ALL SPECIES are FREE,
So SINg your Song little FRoggy,
And ExpERiENCE LoNg Lost HARMony!

Guess how many FROG species are jumping and FLYING throughout the WORLD toDAY?

THREE THOUSAND SEVEN HUNDRED!

The BIGGEST of them ALL is the WEST African GoLiatH FROG. He weighs 10 pounds (4½ kilograms), and jumps 40 times his LeNgth! HE is very strong!

The smallest is the grass frog. These Little frogs are about 1 inch.

Have you heard of the FLYing FROG? The Asiatic GLIDING FROG is KNOWN as the FLYing FROG. He has WEBBED FEET and FLIES from TREE to TREE insiDE the FOREST. She can gLide for DISTANCES of up to 50 feet (15 meters)!

In Ancient EGYPT, the FROG was A symBOL FoR LIFE GIViNg CHaNGE.

South American and INDian people Listen to the FRogs Song as a WAY to KNOW WHEN RAIN is coming.

Every FROG needs WateR to suRVive. Like aLL AmpHiBiaNS, they aBSORB WateR THRough THEIR SKIN.

FRogs Have smooth sLimy SKiN, AND Toads Have RougH DRY SKIN AND usually Live IN DRYer places than the FROG.

In the American InDiAN TraDition, tHE FRog is 'KEEPer of the WateR'.

WateR is HeaLINg AND caN BRING Peace into our Lives.

MaRaDRO ISLaND's FROG, STeVe, says to you, "Go Jump in a Lake, or a stream, or the OCEaN, oR youR BATHTUB, AND SiNg a song! ANy Song!"

Hattie's Café

INVITES

- YOU -
YOUR PICTURE HERE

to join

Radman and Romeo
and friends for a
Sunset to Sunrise
Dance Party!

CELEBRATING
Life
and BEING
ALIVE!

See you there!

Bring tree seeds!

That night, After the Dance Party,
Radman realized one thing . . .

WE ARE the PLants, Animals and People, and THEY aRE US. At that moment RADman MERGeD With ALL CREATION AND FELT At ONE with LIFE Itself.

The Journey never Ends

Romeo and Radman mapping out
their next voyage.

Radman was born on an Island in the South Pacific ⬤cean.
He started traveling to different Island Locations when he
was two years old. His Love for animals and Water have
taken him to faraway places around the World.
He continues to plant trees and help animals and people
Wherever he goes.

Love, Sweet Sweet Love !!!!
This is the Golden Retriever's Nature!
Running free with the Wind, then
Plunging into the Water to Retrieve
the Rock or stick that you throw!
(Romeo has been known to Dive for Rocks,
submerged for up to 40 seconds.)
Golden Retrievers are completely
Devoted to their family and Loved ones,
and guard even the smallest baby with
ultimate Loyalty! They Give, expecting
nothing in return. TRUE LOVE.
Romeo asks, "are you Loyal to your
friends and family?"

TEN LITTLE INDIAN COMMANDMENTS

squawpapaya

TREAT MOTHER EARTH AND ALL THAT LIVE ON EARTH WITH RESPECT.

BE TRUTHFUL AND HONEST AT ALL TIMES.

WORK TOGETHER FOR THE BENEFIT OF PLANTS, ANIMALS AND PEOPLE.

GIVE ASSISTANCE AND KINDNESS WHENEVER NEEDED.

DO WHAT YOU KNOW TO BE RIGHT.

TAKE CARE OF YOUR MIND, BODY AND SOUL.

CONTRIBUTE A SHARE OF YOUR EFFORTS TO WHAT YOU BELIEVE IN.

TAKE FULL RESPONSIBILITY FOR YOUR ACTIONS.

REMAIN CLOSE TO THE GREAT SPIRIT.

FOLLOW YOUR HEART.

Man TREAD gently on sacred ground

Understand, UNDERSTAND what makes the WORLD go around!

Respect ALL creatures great and small,

for as part of the chain, ONE Affects ALL.

We have gone against NATURE and now we see

Our actions have been destructive,

However WE DO KNOW a KEY!

Let us FEED the hungry and DO what WE CAN

To Anyone and EVERYone, PLANT, Animal and MAN.

Mother Nature, Mother Earth, Can you forgive us We Ask?

We will replenish and Nourish you, for that is our task.

Please Let us LISTEN, Be Silent and Still,

for WHEN WE TRULY hear her,

Harmonious ANSWERS will appear.

She is Crying, SHE is Dying, WE have to Start Now

To Love HER, PROtect her, and KNOW How She Works

WHEN WE DO, WE WILL SEE,

ALL WE Have to do is Live COMPASSIONAtely!

Donate time or Money to Organizations You Believe in and Feel Good about!
Here are a few Suggestions.... Look into your Local organizations as WELL!

Friends of the Earth
Global Building
1025 Vermont Avenue
Suite 300
N.W. Washington D.C.
              20005

202·783·7400

Sea Life Park
Turtle Hatchling Program
Marine Education and
Research Foundation
41-202 KaLaniandoLe
Suite 7
Waimanalo, Hawaii
              96795
(808) 259·7933

The American Society
for the Prevention of
   Cruelty to Animals
424 East 92nd Street
New York, New York
          10128-6804
(212) 876·7700

National Audubon Society
700 Broadway
New York, New York 10003
(212) 979·3000

Earthsave
706 Frederick Street
Santa Cruz, California
          95062-2205
(408) 423·4069

Rainforest Action Network
450 Sansome Street
Suite 700
San Francisco, California 94111
(415) 398·4404

Nature Conservancy
570 7th Avenue
Room 601
New York, New York
          10018
(212) 997·1880

World Wildlife Fund
Department ZG11
1250 24th Street
N.W. Washington D.C.
              20037
(202) 293·4800

National Arbor Foundation
211 North 12th Street
Lincoln, Nebraska 68508
(402) 474·5655

World Vision
P.O. Box 1191
Pasadena, California
          91191-0213
(818) 303·8811

National Wildlife
Federation
1400 Sixteenth Street
N.W. Washington D.C.
          20036-2266
(202) 797·6800

Unicef Childrens Fund
U.S. Committee
333 East 38th Street
New York, New York
              10016
(212) 686·5522

Sierra Club
2nd Floor
85 2nd Street
San Francisco
California 94105
(415) 977·5500

National Resources
Defense Council
40 West 20th Street
New York, New York
              10011
(212) 727·2700

Childrens Defense Fund
25 E. Street
N.W. Washington D.C.
              20001
(202) 628·8787

Greenpeace
1436 U. Street
N.W. Washington D.C.
              20009
(202) 462·1177

Whales Alive
P.O. Box 2058
Kihei, Hawaii
          96753
(808) 874·6855

a portion of the profits from this Book are Donated to organizations Worldwide.

CELEBRATE Life!

FOR iN LiFE

ANything

is possible! ☆

Go forth and CReate
things that ꞏYOUꞏ KNOW
are for the
GooD of ALL
PLaNts, Animals and PEople!